PADRE PIO
SAINT PIUS OF PIETRELCINA

CTS Children's Books

Contents

Text by Francesca Fabris
Illustrations by Tommaso D'Incalci
Translated by Matthew Sherry

Padre Pio - Saint Pius of Pietrelcina: Published 2013 by The Incorporated Catholic Truth Society, 40-46 Harleyford Road, London SE11 5AY. Tel: 020 7640 0042; Fax: 020 7640 0046; www.CTSbooks.org Copyright © 2013 The Incorporated Catholic Truth Society in this English-language edition.

ISBN: 978 1 86082 889 8   CTS Code CH 50

Translated from the original Italian Edition **San Pio da Pietrelcina** - ISBN 978-88-6124-219-7, published by Il Pozzo di Giacobbe, Gruppo Editoriale S.R.L., Cortile San Teodoro, 3, 91100 Trapani (TP), Italy © 2013 Il Pozzo di Giacobbe.

HIS NAME WAS FRANCESCO

Pietrelcina is a little town in the province of Benevento in the south of Italy. Its name comes from Petra Pucina, which means 'little rock.' In the old part of town, the homes are built on the rock and the people walk on the rocky streets instead of pavements. It is a little hillside town where the people live a simple life of farming.

This is where Saint Pio was born. His father and mother were humble farmers. Their names were Maria Giuseppa Forgione and Grazio Forgione, and on 25th May 1887 they were overjoyed at the birth of a beautiful baby boy. They named him Francesco. So the first name Saint Pio ever had was Francesco Forgione. He would change it later, when he entered the friary.

A YOUNG SHEPHERD

Francesco was a calm and quiet child. He grew up in humble surroundings, among kind and orderly people, in touch with the rhythms of nature. He quickly learned the meaning of sacrifice.

Every morning his father would open a trapdoor that led from the bedroom to the stable, climb down the stairs, lead the donkey outside, and go to work in the fields. He ploughed the earth, sowed seeds, and harvested crops from sunrise to sunset. He was a tireless worker, and he was able to grow enough food to feed his family. Papà Grazio may not have been able to read or write, but he was very wise.

He was always cheerful and he often sang, with a happy heart. He was also very sensitive, and if he happened to find any living creatures while he was breaking up the ground, instead of killing them he would carefully pick them up and set them aside.

4

Francesco watched everything that his father did, and without realising it he learned to respect life and be honest and serious.

Until he was ten years old Francesco did not go to school, but took the family's little flock of sheep to pasture. In the morning his mother would prepare a slice of bread for his breakfast, wrapped up in a clean napkin. He would sit down, open the napkin in his lap, and eat without hurrying. If any crumbs fell on the grass, he would pick them up and eat them right away, as a sign of respect for the bread that is a gift from God.

BUILDING A CHRISTMAS CRIB

F rancesco did not have many friends, but he did have one special friend named Luigi. He was a shepherd, too.

While the sheep were grazing in the grass, the two friends would play in the fields. They were always cheerful and carefree, playfighting, playing tricks on each other, and even playing some little pranks with the other children.

Like all children, Francesco loved Christmas. He would wait eagerly for the celebration, and he especially liked to set up the crib. His friends' parents usually helped them with their Nativity scenes, but Papà Grazio did not have much time to devote to his son, so Francesco did the best he could.

Back then they could not buy figurines at a shop, so they had to make do with the materials available: a few stones, some pine cones from the forest, sticks, moss and clay - that was enough to make all of the characters and scenery.

There was no electricity in Pietrelcina, so the children had learned to make oil lamps using snail shells, and they decorated the Nativity scenes with these so that they would be lit up at night.

Francesco's crib may not have been as colourful as those of children today, but it was certainly cared for just as well.

It is said that Francesco especially loved to model the figurines with his own hands. He wanted to mould them until they were as beautiful as he could make them, especially the Baby Jesus. He would shape the clay and then press it smooth and shape it again, until he was satisfied with the result.

FRANCESCO RECEIVES HIS CALLING

After Francesco turned ten he began to study. This was what his parents wanted, and he was also curious to learn new things. His parents found a priest nearby who no longer served at any parish. He offered to give private lessons, so Francesco learned to read, write, and do arithmetic.

But things did not go so well with this first teacher, so his parents decided to find him another. With the new teacher Francesco showed great seriousness and determination, and the results were fairly good.

As a little boy he learned to love prayer. His family was very devout, and they recited the Rosary together every evening in the kitchen.

Francesco also prayed very often on his own, and in this dialogue with God he found comfort and relief.

8

Of course, it was the atmosphere of his family, sensitive to the call of God, that brought out the vocation to religious life in him. But there was also another person in Francesco's life who made him curious and gave him the desire to get to know the life in the friary better. His name was Camillo, and he was a young friar who had come to town begging for alms in the street.

Francesco liked Camillo, because he was very nice and always cheerful. And Francesco wanted to be like him. When he was fourteen, he told his parents that he wanted to become a friar. Papà Grazio was very happy about this decision, but his family was very poor and in order to pay for his education his father went to America to look for work, because what he earned in Pietrelcina was not enough to send his son to private school.

FRANCESCO CHANGES HIS NAME

When Francesco's uncle learned about his decision, he suggested various religious orders: the Cistercians, the Redemptorists, the Franciscans.... Before choosing one, Francesco wanted to know if they would let him grow his beard long, because he wanted to be like Brother Camillo in everything, even in his beard! So on 22nd January 1903, at the age of sixteen, Francesco entered the friary of the Capuchin Franciscans.

At the end of the novitiate, when he became a friar, he had to change his name to show that he had started a new life.

He decided to call himself Pio, and instead of his last name he took the name of his town, Pietrelcina. Now Francesco Forgione became Padre Pio of Pietrelcina.

And this is how he is remembered today.

Life in the friary had strict and austere rules, especially that of absolute poverty according to the spirit of Saint Francis, but Padre Pio adapted to it easily. On 27th January 1907 he made his solemn vows of poverty, chastity, and obedience, and three years later he became a priest. He wanted to leave immediately as a missionary and travel to faraway lands, to bring the Gospel and the words of Jesus to the ends of the earth, but we will see that life would take him elsewhere. To the place where God wanted him.

The first years of Padre Pio's priesthood were troubled by health problems: unfortunately, he suffered from a lung disease. His superiors sent him several times to Pietrelcina, where the climate was better and could help him to get healthy.

IN A SOLITARY LITTLE HOUSE

The rules of the Capuchins were unbreakable: anyone who had to be away from the friary for a long time could not go back to his family, or he would have to give up the garments of Saint Francis. In order to follow this rule, his parents rented him a room close to their house.

It was a little house built on the rock, that stood on the ruins of the ancient castle of Pietrelcina, called La Torretta.

In the wintertime Padre Pio lived in the Torretta, while in the summertime he moved to a cabin that stayed cooler inside. Papà Grazio had built this cabin in Piana Romana, near the elm tree his son liked so much.

During these years Padre Pio was able to reflect, write to his spiritual fathers, and find comfort in his many sufferings, not only physical but spiritual as well. He was tormented by temptations, and he overcame these by turning to Jesus, whom he always felt close to him, to the Blessed Mother, who was like a mother full of tenderness and always beside him, to Saint Francis, and to the guardian angel who gave him strength and courage.

He also had the support of his family and fellow townspeople, who showed him a great deal of affection. As well as his serious sufferings, Padre Pio also had wonderful and serene moments in Pietrelcina, which would prepare him for the mission that the Lord had in mind for him: that of making himself available for his brethren, to make known to all the love of the good Father.

13

IN THE CONFESSIONAL

To lead souls back to God: this would be his mission.

Padre Pio heard something like a voice inside him saying, "Make yourself holy, and make others holy!" He meditated on these words and prayed, asking the Lord to enlighten him about their meaning.

And he understood that his task for the future would be that of being a sign of God's forgiveness, who like an immensely good Father welcomes in his embrace all those who return to him with a repentant heart.

Jesus had said, "Healthy people do not need the doctor, but sick people do. I have not come to call the just, but sinners."

14

The sick that Jesus was talking about are people who have made mistakes and committed sins, and the doctor is the priest who can forgive them, showing the merciful face of God. He then remembered a beautiful speech that Agostino, his spiritual father, had given on the occasion of the first Mass Padre Pio celebrated when he became a priest.

Among the many other things he had said, Father Agostino had made the best prayer possible for him: that he would become a good confessor.

Like Simon of Cyrene, who had helped the suffering Jesus to carry his cross, so Padre Pio wanted to become the Cyrenian of humanity and bring help to suffering Christians, lifting the burden of the evil they had done.

THE PASSION OF JESUS

Padre Pio's superiors decided to transfer him to San Giovanni Rotondo. This is a little town in the province of Foggia, in the Gargano, the site of the friary of the Capuchin Franciscans dedicated to Saint Mary of Graces. Padre Pio arrived there on 28th July 1916, and would stay there for the rest of his life.

On 20th September 1918 something extraordinary happened to Pio: he received the stigmata of the passion of Jesus, an exceptional event that has rarely happened in the history of the saints. Padre Pio was praying in the chapel, and he started to feel drowsy. After he fell asleep, he saw a man who had wounds on his hands, feet, and side, like those of Jesus on the cross. He was losing blood, and at the mere sight of this man Padre Pio became very afraid. Then he felt sensations that are hard to describe. He felt like he was dying. He remained unconscious for a long time. When he woke up, he was in a lot of pain and he saw that there were wounds on his hands, his feet, and his side. Padre Pio tried to hide what had happened to him, but the news spread quickly not only among his fellow Franciscans, but also outside of the friary. And San Giovanni Rotondo became a destination for many pilgrims.

17

A DESTINATION FOR PILGRIMS

From this time on, many faithful came to visit Padre Pio. They knew they were going to see a saint. Some came for confession, some for advice or a word of encouragement. Everyone felt loved by him. In his letters he wrote: "I am devoured by love of God and love of neighbour." He prayed tirelessly to lead his brethren back to God; he always remembered everyone in his silent prayer. To him, everything belonged to God and must return to him. His friends had the privilege of being remembered while he was celebrating Mass.

He never tired of asking for intercession for the salvation of souls. In his heart he placed all of his friends on the altar to offer them to the tenderness of God.

The confessional became his world, he was untiring. The greatest gift he could give to humanity was to free believers from their sins and lead them back, purified, to God. In this he showed himself as a father to all, good and understanding toward every kind of misfortune.

He loved to see sincerity of heart in the faithful. This meant he could be the instrument of Jesus's mercy. People were eager to see him because he made them feel better. Everyone admired and trusted him. They were convinced he was a saint even then.

Many people wrote him letters full of affection, and he responded with great emotion. He loved to receive messages and care for souls even by post! There were also some who did not believe and wanted to see with their own eyes if the stigmata were real or if Padre Pio had made everything up. But those who came to him with doubts went away changed, with their hearts full of tenderness.

THE HOME FOR THE RELIEF OF THE SUFFERING

Padre Pio lived his poverty to the full. He never wanted new clothes, he was content wearing used clothing. He lived in his cell, which was humble and bare. He needed very little to be happy: an altar to celebrate the mysteries of God and a confessional for caring for souls.

A lot of money passed through his hands, given to him by good people who made many donations, because they knew that with him their treasures were safe and that he would use them for the needy.

In fact, Padre Pio used the money to build the Home for the Relief of the Suffering, a very important hospital, because the sick were so dear to his heart.

Padre Pio died in San Giovanni Rotondo on 23rd September 1968. On 16th June 2002 he was proclaimed a saint by Pope John Paul II. His feast is celebrated on 23rd September.

Padre Pio of Pietrelcina was a humble Capuchin priest from an isolated friary in Puglia, but thanks to his spirituality and his holiness he is now known all over the world. The friary of San Giovanni Rotondo, in fact, has become very famous. Its crypt contains the remains of Padre Pio, and it receives millions of devout visitors every year.

A SPECIAL SIGN

Saint Francis of Assisi had also received the stigmata, in 1224. But what is the meaning of this for Christians?

The stigmata are a sign of the passion of Jesus, and all who see them remember the decision of Jesus to love us completely. He went to his death in order to save us, and although he did this two thousand years ago, the love of Jesus for humanity remains unchanged even today.

A person who receives the stigmata is a sign of God's faithful love for humanity that endures even today.

"Pray and hope.
God is merciful and
he will hear your prayer."

Padre Pio

AN IMAGE OF
PADRE PIO

23

A PRAYER
OF PADRE PIO

O holy Guardian Angel,

take care of my soul

and my body.

Enlighten my mind

so that I may know the Lord better

and love him with all my heart.

Assist me in my prayers,

so that I may not give in to distraction,

but give them my greatest attention.

Help me with your advice,

so that I may see what is good

and do it with generosity.